Contents

2	Place value	**26**	C
4	Numbers up to 1000	**28**	N
6	Mental addition	**30**	T
8	Mental subtraction	**32**	Angles
10	Addition	**34**	Straight lines
12	Subtraction	**36**	2D shapes
14	Multiples	**38**	3D shapes
16	Multiplication	**40**	Statistics
18	Division	**42**	Quick test
20	Fractions	**44**	Explorer's logbook
22	Length	**46**	Answers
24	Weight		

Introduction

If you are wild about learning and wild about animals – this book is for you! It will take you on a wild adventure, where you will practise key maths skills and explore the amazing world of baby animals along the way.

Each maths topic is introduced in a clear and simple way, with lots of interesting activities to complete, so that you can practise what you have learned.

You should attempt the tasks without a calculator unless instructed otherwise, but calculators may be used to check your answers.

Alongside every topic, you will discover fascinating facts about baby animals.

Animal babies often have strange names.

What is your favourite baby animal?

When you have completed each topic, record the animals that you have seen and the skills that you have learned in the explorer's logbook on pages 44–45.

Good luck, explorer!

Pamela Wild

Place value

A number can only be made up from the digits 1 2 3 4 5 6 7 8 9 and 0 (zero).

A digit's value (what it is worth) depends on which column it is placed in.

H T U

		1	This 1 is in the units column and is worth just 1
	1	0	This 1 is in the tens column and is worth one set of 10
1	0	0	This 1 is in the hundreds column and is worth one set of 100

Zero is used as a place holder so that we know which column a digit is in when there are no column headings.

Task 1 Write down the value of the underlined digit.

a 49<u>2</u> _____

b <u>5</u>63 _____

c 2<u>9</u>0 _____

d 80<u>6</u> _____

e 3<u>5</u>9 _____

f <u>3</u>04 _____

Write down the numbers represented here.

a

b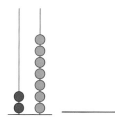

c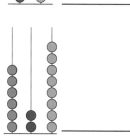

d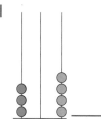

Task 3 Draw circles in the appropriate columns to represent these numbers.

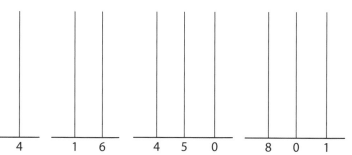

| 3 | 4 | | 1 | 6 | | 4 | 5 | 0 | | 8 | 0 | 1 |

Exploring Further ...

Help the puppies reach their mum. In the table below write down how many units, tens and hundreds are needed to get from the first number to the last number. The first one has been done for you.

	First number	Hundreds	Tens	Units	Last number
🐶	150		1	6	166
🐶	540				597
🐶	610				681
🐶	320				763
🐶	430				658

Now spring to pages 44–45 to record what you have learned in your explorer's logbook.

3

Numbers up to 1000

Understanding the place value of numbers helps us to read, write, compare and order them.

Which number is bigger?
458   or   485

Discover how well you can do this and check whether you can count in ones, tens and hundreds.

WILD FACT

From about two weeks old, kittens' legs are strong enough to walk and run. They love to play, fight and explore their world. If their mother thinks they are in danger though, she will pick them up in her mouth and carry them to safety.

FACT FILE

Animal: Kitten
Habitat: Domestic habitat
Weight: At 4 weeks they are about 0.36 kg
Lifespan: 15 to 17 years for domesticated cats
Diet: Mother's milk for first 3 to 4 weeks, then cat food

Task 1   Write these numbers in words.

a 43 _____

b 91 _____

c 258 _____

d 707 _____

Task 2
Write these numbers in figures.

a seventy-seven _____

b six hundred and eighteen _____

c nine hundred and ninety-nine _____

Task 3
Order these numbers from biggest to smallest.

a 405   540   450   504   545   454

_____

Order these numbers from smallest to biggest.

b 111   101   110   11   121   211

_____

Task 4
Fill in the gaps in the number sequences.

a 169   [   ]   171   172   [   ]   [   ]

b 581   591   [   ]   [   ]   [   ]   [   ]

Exploring Further ...

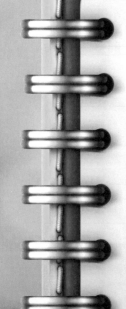

a Make the biggest number you can using these three digits. _____

b Make the smallest number you can using these three digits. _____

c Make the number that is closest to 800. _____

Now tumble to pages 44–45 to record what you have learned in your explorer's logbook.

Mental addition

FACT FILE

Animal: Foal (baby horse)
Habitat: Open, grassy areas with water nearby
Weight: Average 35 kg at birth
Lifespan: 25 to 30 years
Diet: Mother's milk for first 6 to 8 weeks, then hay, grass and grains

WILD FACT

Foals seem to be all legs. In fact, when they are born their legs only have to grow a bit more to reach adult length. They need long legs to reach their mother's milk. Most foals are born at night or very early in the morning.

Task 1 — Add these numbers in your head.

a 851 + 3 + 4 _____

b 673 + 5 + 2 _____

c 955 + 4 + 4 _____

d 307 + 4 + 2 _____

e 224 + 5 + 2 _____

f 713 + 3 + 3 _____

g 901 + 4 + 2 _____

h 364 + 5 + 1 _____

Task 2 — Add these numbers in your head.

a 432 + 20 + 30 _____

b 126 + 60 + 10 _____

c 250 + 40 + 10 _____

d 364 + 30 + 50 _____

e 622 + 30 + 10 _____

f 519 + 20 + 20 _____

g 304 + 50 + 30 _____

h 792 + 10 + 40 _____

Task 3 — Now add these bigger numbers in your head.

a 481 + 400 _____

b 601 + 300 _____

c 236 + 600 + 100 _____

d 103 + 100 + 700 _____

WILD FACT

Did you know that a foal can stand an hour after birth and can walk, trot and run just two hours after birth? Amazing! In the wild it is important that a foal is safe from predators, so it needs to move fairly quickly after birth. It also needs to stand to feed from its mother.

Exploring Further ...

Discover the name of Liz's foal. Colour the answer to each of these sums and the name will be revealed.

208	965	160	17	395	58	471	178	36	47	729	28	653
909	398	492	56	824	25	57	93	97	798	74	30	67
27	48	86	593	92	77	54	149	91	207	772	229	41
643	81	741	19	62	482	87	150	903	712	797	845	78
45	68	88	663	303	999	697	6	85	505	228	99	37

33 + 4 = ?	21 + 7 = ?	63 + 34 = ?	157 + 3 = ?	472 + 300 = ?
65 + 2 = ?	52 + 6 = ?	35 + 22 = ?	298 + 5 = ?	609 + 300 = ?
76 + 1 = ?	43 + 5 = ?	46 + 41 = ?	645 + 8 = ?	297 + 500 = ?
47 + 7 = ?	19 + 8 = ?	57 + 17 = ?	725 + 4 = ?	865 + 100 = ?
85 + 7 = ?	78 + 8 = ?	25 + 37 = ?	203 + 5 = ?	341 + 400 = ?
34 + 7 = ?	37 + 8 = ?	74 + 17 = ?	335 + 60 = ?	421 + 50 = ?
41 + 27 = ?	62 + 16 = ?	53 + 35 = ?	617 + 80 = ?	784 + 40 = ?
29 + 18 = ?	18 + 18 = ?	57 + 28 = ?	813 + 90 = ?	158 + 70 = ?

Now trot to pages 44–45 to record what you have learned in your explorer's logbook.

Mental subtraction

Subtracting in your head is a bit harder than adding.

You can either take away the smaller number from the bigger one:

68 – 5 = 63

or you can add from the smaller number to the bigger one to find the difference:

74 – 46 = 28

Practise your number bonds! If you know that 8 + 9 = 17, then you also know that 17 – 8 = 9 and 17 – 9 = 8.

Task 1   Subtract these numbers in your head.

a 764 – 3 _____   **b** 809 – 2 _____

c 722 – 8 _____   **d** 936 – 7 _____

e 792 – 30 _____   **f** 561 – 50 _____

g 482 – 90 _____   **h** 353 – 70 _____

Task 2

Now subtract these bigger numbers in your head.

a 295 – 100 _____

b 612 – 300 _____

c 750 – 400 _____

d 901 – 600 _____

WILD FACT

It takes six weeks for the eggs to hatch and another two to three months before the eaglet leaves the nest.

Task 3

Solve these problems in your head.

a There used to be 698 eagles in the United Kingdom. Scientists think that 90 have died or been killed. How many eagles are left? _____

b It took 108 days from when an eagle's egg was laid to the eaglet leaving the nest. If it took 43 days for the egg to hatch, how long was the baby bird in the nest before it took its first flight? _____

c If 37 out of a total of 81 eagles in Scotland are male, how many are female? _____

WILD FACT

The mother usually lays two eggs. Sadly the second one to hatch is often eaten by the older chick. Even if it is not eaten, the younger chick will probably starve because its brother or sister eats most of the food.

Exploring Further ...

83   29   37   33   62   54

a Which two pairs of numbers have a difference of 21?

_____

b Which number is 17 less than 54? _____

c Which number is the answer to 62 minus 29? _____

d What is left when 29 is subtracted from 83? _____

Now fly to pages 44–45 to record what you have learned in your explorer's logbook.

Addition

Addition puts two or more groups of things together. Do you know all the words for add?

sum, total, altogether, plus, increase

Sometimes the calculation is too hard to complete in your head, and that's when you use a formal method.

Can you use the columnar method for adding?

H	T	U
3	1	8
+ 5	9	6
9	1	4
1	1	

Task 1 Complete these sums using the columnar method.

a 38 + 47

b 86 plus 93

c What is the total of 24, 8 and 57?

d Increase 63 by 38

Task 2   Use the columnar method to add.

a   306
    + 659
    _____

    _____

b   284
    + 45
    _____

    _____

c   3
     268
    + 39
    _____

    _____

d   3
      74
    + 528
    _____

    _____

WILD FACT

Cygnets feathers are a drab grey colour which later changes to brown. They do not grow adult plumage until they are over a year old when they then become the most beautiful of water birds.

Task 3   Solve the word problem using the columnar method.

The charity *Look After the Birds* has three bird reserves. Scientists think that 134 cygnets were born at Reserve One, 289 at Reserve Two and 68 at Reserve Three. How many cygnets were born altogether at the three reserves?

WILD FACT

Cygnets leave the nest soon after hatching but stay with their parents for several months before going off on their own. They often curl up inside their parent's folded wings and can be seen hitching a ride as the parent swims along.

Exploring Further ...

Help the swans to find their cygnet. Each swan must step onto one square from each column to make the total on her cygnet's square.

Swan A 364	306	83	Cygnet B 886
Swan B 497	47	109	Cygnet C 495
Swan C 59	327	258	Cygnet A 669

Now glide to pages 44-45 to record what you have learned in your explorer's logbook.

Subtraction

Animal:	Joey (baby kangaroo)
Habitat:	Woods and bushlands of Australia
Weight:	1 g at birth
Lifespan:	12 to 18 years in the wild
Diet:	Mother's milk inside the pouch, later eats grass shoots and leaves

Subtraction lets us find out how many are left or how much more/less there is of one thing than another. Subtraction is the opposite process to addition.

$5 + 4 = 9$ — Subtraction can undo this addition: $9 - 4 = 5$

$7 - 3 = 4$ — Addition can undo this subtraction: $3 + 4 = 7$

Make sure you know your subtraction vocabulary: **take away, subtract, find the difference, how many more, how many less, decrease**.

Discover how well you understand the columnar method!

H	T	U		H	T	U
8	4	7		$^6\!7$	$^{11}\!2$	$^1\!5$
− 5	4	3		− 2	9	6
3	0	4		4	2	9

Task 1 — Use the columnar method to complete these subtractions.

a 836 take away 30

b Find the difference between 15 and 927

Task 2 Use the columnar method to complete these subtractions.

a 43 minus 16

b What is 47 less than 92?

c Subtract 38 from 70

d Take 53 from 384

Task 3 Subtract these numbers using the columnar method.

a
738
− 453
_____

b
624
− 54
_____

c
901
− 690
_____

d
834
− 795
_____

Exploring Further ...

Three joeys have a jumping competition. Find the answers to these problems using the columnar method.

1
203 cm

2
176 cm

3
251 cm

a How much further does Joey 1 jump than Joey 2?

b What is the difference in length between Joey 3's jump and Joey 1's jump?

Now jump to pages 44–45 to record what you have learned in your explorer's logbook.

13

Multiples

A **multiple** represents a set or sets of a number.

2, 4, 6, 8, 10, 12, 14, 16, 18 and 20 are sets of 2. They are multiples of 2.

5, 10, 15, 20 are sets of 5. They are multiples of 5.

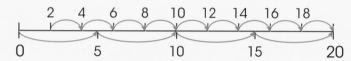

You need to know your times tables to work with multiples accurately.

FACT FILE

Animal: Tadpole

Habitat: Just below the surface of shallow waters such as lakes, ponds and streams

Lifespan: At around 12 weeks the tadpole has grown into a frog

Diet: Underwater plants and algae, eats small insects once it is older

WILD FACT

Frogspawn is a mass of 2000 to 4000 eggs laid by a female frog. At first, the tadpole is a tiny dot inside the egg. By feeding on the yolk sac, the tadpole grows and its black tail can be seen inside the egg.

Task 1 Track down the missing multiples.

a	18	20			26	28		
b	18			27	30		36	
c		20		28	32		40	
d	15	20				40	45	

14

| Task 2 | Underline the numbers that are: |

a multiples of 10:   20   45   54   60   30   100

b multiples of 8:   24   48   80   74   54   96

c multiples of 4 and 8:   20   8   28   48   32   54

d multiples of 2 and 3:   9   12   15   20   27   30

e multiples of 5 and 10:   25   50   60   15   10   45

f multiples of 50 and 100:   50   150   100   250   200   600

| Task 3 | Work out the number that each frog is thinking of. |

a 'My number is a multiple of 5 and 2. It lies between 25 and 35.' _____

b 'My number is a multiple of 8. It is a two-digit number. The two digits add up to make 9.' _____

WILD FACT

After 10 days the tadpole comes out of the egg with a tail and fins, breathing through gills like a fish. During the next 10 to 12 weeks its legs grow, its tail disappears and lungs replace the gills. The tadpole is now a young frog and can leave the water. What a clever transformation!

Exploring Further ...

Help each tadpole to become a frog.
Tadpole 1 moves along multiples of 8.
Tadpole 2 moves along multiples of 5.
Tadpole 3 moves along numbers that are multiples of both 2 and 3.

1	55	14	15	104	27	18	35	A
2	32	95	36	40	30	85	42	B
3	12	24	88	6	56	16	64	C

Now swim to pages 44–45 to record what you have learned in your explorer's logbook.

15

Multiplication

Multiplication is the repeated addition of a number.

It is represented by the sign ×.

6 × 3 can be worked out as 6 sets of 3 (3 + 3 + 3 + 3 + 3 + 3)
or 3 sets of 6 (6 + 6 + 6)

If you know the multiplication fact 6 × 3 = 18 or 3 × 6 = 18, it makes life a lot easier – so learn your tables!

Do you know all the words for multiply?

times, sets of, product

You also should know how to use more formal methods of multiplication so that you can deal with bigger numbers.

The cross method: 67 × 3

	7 ×	60 ×	67 ×
3	21	180	201

The columnar method:

T	U
6	7
×	3
2 0	1

2

Task 1 How well do you know your multiplication facts?

a **i** 3 × 2 = ☐ **ii** 3 × 5 = ☐ **iii** 4 × 3 = ☐ **iv** 6 × 3 = ☐

b **i** 9 × 2 = ☐ **ii** 5 × 4 = ☐ **iii** 2 × 8 = ☐ **iv** 11 × 2 = ☐

c **i** 7 × 4 = ☐ **ii** 8 × 5 = ☐ **iii** 7 × 8 = ☐ **iv** 8 × 3 = ☐

Task 2 Complete these multiplication sums using the cross method.

a 84 × 8

	4 ×	80 ×	84 ×
8			

b 75 × 2

	5 ×	70 ×	75 ×
2			

Task 3

Complete these multiplication sums using the columnar method.

a   89
   × 5
 _____

b   37
   × 8
 _____

c   46
   × 4
 _____

d   94
   × 3
 _____

FACT FILE

Animal: Hoglet (baby hedgehog)
Habitat: Woodland habitats, fields, parks and gardens
Weight: 110 to 170g at 3 to 4 weeks old
Lifespan: Up to 6 years
Diet: Mother's milk for first 4 to 6 weeks, then insects and slugs

Task 4

Investigate multiplying a multiple of ten.

a $60 \times 8 =$ _____   b $80 \times 4 =$ _____

c $70 \times 5 =$ _____   d $50 \times 4 =$ _____

Exploring Further ...

Solve these word problems. In each case write down the sum you used to calculate the answer.

a   A baby hedgehog is 7 cm long. When fully grown it will be four times this length. What length will it grow to?

   _____

b   I drew a sketch of a hedgehog and made it five times smaller than the actual size. If my drawing is 6 cm, what was the size of the real hedgehog? _____

c   Paul has four anoraks and five scarves for countryside walks. He likes to wear a different combination each time he goes out. How many different outfits can he wear?

   _____

Now roll to pages 44–45 to record what you have learned in your explorer's logbook.

Division

FACT FILE

Animal: Duckling

Habitat: Ponds, streams and lakes

Weight: 36 g after a day but 50 g two days later!

Lifespan: 5 to 10 years in the wild

Diet: Insects, snails, sea grass and vegetation

There are two questions you can ask yourself when **dividing**.

Look at the sum $6 \div 2$.

You can ask: 'What is 6 shared between 2?'

$6 \div 2 = 3$

Or you can ask: 'How many sets of 2 in 6?'

$6 \div 2 = 3$

Whichever question you ask, the answer will be the same.

Discover how well you can use the formal written method for division.

$75 \div 5$

WILD FACT

A duckling's journey to water can be very dangerous but is necessary as the water is the safest place and provides their food.

Task 1   How well do you know your division facts?

a i $60 \div 5 =$ ☐   ii $48 \div 8 =$ ☐   iii $20 \div 2 =$ ☐   iv $27 \div 3 =$ ☐

b i $24 \div 4 =$ ☐   ii $24 \div 3 =$ ☐   iii $24 \div 8 =$ ☐   iv $24 \div 2 =$ ☐

c i $35 \div 5 =$ ☐   ii $32 \div 4 =$ ☐   iii $56 \div 8 =$ ☐   iv $40 \div 5 =$ ☐

d i $72 \div 8 =$ ☐   ii $18 \div 3 =$ ☐   iii $16 \div 4 =$ ☐   iv $14 \div 2 =$ ☐

Task 2

Investigate dividing a multiple of 10.

a $80 \div 4 =$ _____

b $90 \div 3 =$ _____

c $240 \div 8 =$ _____

d $300 \div 5 =$ _____

e $400 \div 4 =$ _____

f $600 \div 3 =$ _____

g $100 \div 5 =$ _____

h $350 \div 2 =$ _____

WILD FACT

Ducklings are active as soon as they hatch, and within 10 hours their mother leads them to the nearest water. Ducklings are dependent on their mothers for about 60 days after hatching.

Task 3

Use the formal written method to solve these divisions.

a $68 \div 2$

b $93 \div 3$

c $84 \div 2$

d $60 \div 3$

e $92 \div 4$

f $104 \div 8$

Exploring Further ...

Saima, Jack, Millie and Lee went for a picnic. They took 16 sandwiches, 8 apples, 32 grapes, 2 packets of crisps and 4 biscuits. They shared the food equally amongst the four of them. How many of each item did each child receive?

Sandwiches _____   Apples _____   Grapes _____

Packet of crisps _____   Biscuits _____

Now paddle to pages 44–45 to record what you have learned in your explorer's logbook.

Fractions

A fraction is part of a whole one.

This bar has been divided into five equal parts.

$\frac{1}{5}$	$\frac{1}{5}$	$\frac{1}{5}$	$\frac{1}{5}$	$\frac{1}{5}$

Each part is one-fifth of the whole bar: $\frac{1}{5}$.

The number below the line – the **denominator** – tells us how many parts the whole one has been divided into.

If I take two equal parts, I will have two-fifths: $\frac{2}{5}$

The number above the line – the **numerator** – tells us how many equal parts we have.

Task 1 When a whole one is divided into 10 equal parts, each part is called one-tenth or $\frac{1}{10}$.

$\frac{1}{10}$	$\frac{1}{10}$	$\frac{1}{10}$	$\frac{1}{10}$	$\frac{1}{10}$	$\frac{1}{10}$	$\frac{1}{10}$	$\frac{1}{10}$	$\frac{1}{10}$	$\frac{1}{10}$

How many tenths have been shaded and left unshaded in each diagram? Write in words (e.g. one-tenth) and in figures (e.g. $\frac{1}{10}$).

a

Shaded?   Words: _____   Figures:

Unshaded? Words: _____   Figures:

b

Shaded?   Words: _____   Figures:

Unshaded? Words: _____   Figures:

Seal pups quickly put on weight because their mothers' milk is rich in fat. A layer of blubber forms underneath the skin. This is essential for staying warm in the sea.

Task 2 Write down the fraction of seal pups that have been circled.

a _____

b _____

Task 3 Put < (is less than) or > (is more than) between these fractions.

a $\frac{1}{2}$ ☐ $\frac{1}{3}$ b $\frac{1}{4}$ ☐ $\frac{1}{5}$ c $\frac{1}{8}$ ☐ $\frac{1}{6}$ d $\frac{2}{7}$ ☐ $\frac{2}{3}$

Exploring Further ...

a The bucket had 12 fish in it. There are now 3 fish remaining. Write down the fraction of fish eaten by the seal pup.

b The bucket had 9 fish in it. The seal pup has eaten 3 fish. Write down the fraction of fish left in the bucket.

$\frac{3}{12} = \frac{}{12}$

$\frac{}{9} = \frac{3}{9}$

Now splash to pages 44–45 to record what you have learned in your explorer's logbook.

Length

We measure **length** (how long or how far away) in standard units called **millimetres (mm)**, **centimetres (cm)**, **metres (m)** and **kilometres (km)**. Check whether you know these facts:

10 mm = 1 cm
100 cm = 1 m

Check that you can measure accurately with a ruler or tape measure too.

FACT FILE

Animal:	Panda cub
Habitat:	Mountain ranges in central China
Weight:	About 100 to 200 g at birth
Lifespan:	Giant wild pandas live 15 to 20 years on average
Diet:	Fed milk by their mother until about 9 months old

WILD FACT

Pandas usually give birth to just one cub. The cubs stay with their mother for about 18 months and some choose to remain for longer.

Task 1	What are the measurements on this ruler?

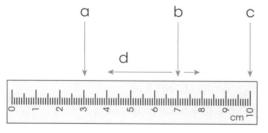

a _____   b _____

c _____   d _____

Estimate how long these creatures are. Then measure **a** in millimetres and **b** and **c** in centimetres.

a _____

b _____

c _____

Task 3   Now try these questions.

29 cm   83 cm   14 cm   47 cm

a How much longer is the otter than the rabbit? _____

b What is the total length of all four animals? _____

c What is the difference between the lengths of the water vole and the rabbit? _____

Exploring Further ...

Join each animal to a suitable equal length in both the top and the bottom row.

4 cm   150 mm   50 cm   20 mm   2 m   100 cm

15 cm   2 cm   40 mm $\frac{1}{2}$ m   1 m   200 cm

Now clamber to pages 44–45 to record what you have learned in your explorer's logbook.

Weight

We measure **weight** or **mass** (how heavy something is) in standard units called **milligrams (mg)**, **grams (g)**, **kilograms (kg)** and **tonnes (t)**. These facts are really easy to remember:

1000 mg = 1 g

1000 g = 1 kg

1000 kg = 1 tonne

FACT FILE

Animal: Fawn (baby deer)

Habitat: Woodlands, mountains and grasslands

Weight: White-tailed fawns weigh up to 4.5 kg at birth

Lifespan: 4 to 10 years

Diet: Mother's milk for the first few weeks; at 6 weeks they start to eat vegetation

Task 1	Match each animal to the most suitable unit to measure weight.

cygnet

newborn joey

foal

1g

1kg

baby elephant

fawn

hoglet

Task 2 Change these grams into kilograms.

a 1000 g _____ b 2000 g _____

c 7000 g _____ d 3000 g _____

e 6000 g _____ f 4000 g _____

Change these kilograms into grams.

g 6 kg _____ h 5 kg _____

i $\frac{1}{2}$ kg _____ j 2 kg _____

k 1 kg _____ l 7 kg _____

WILD FACT

Like foals, a fawn can stand about half an hour after its birth. Within a few days it can outrun a human. However, fawns spend a lot of their early days hiding in the long grass while their mothers graze.

Task 3 Put these weights in order, starting with the heaviest.

 4 kg    1400 g   2000 g   3500 g   6 kg

_____

WILD FACT

Fawns are born with about 300 white spots on their coats. These disappear at about five months old.

Exploring Further ...

a Colour the matching weights in this grid. Use a different colour for each pair.

2020 g	141 g	2 kg 202 g	2220 g	2002 g
2 kg 200 g	2 kg 22 g	2200 g	2 kg 20 g	557 g
402 g	2 kg 2 g	2202 g	2022 g	2 kg 220 g

b What is the total of the three weights left? _____

c Put an arrow on the scale to show this weight.

0 g   500 g   1 kg   1.5 kg   2 kg   2.5 kg   3 kg

Now lope to pages 44–45 to record what you have learned in your explorer's logbook.

Capacity

FACT FILE

Animal:	Black bear cub
Habitat:	Mostly found in forests with plenty of vegetation
Weight:	About 0.35 kg at birth
Lifespan:	20 years in the wild
Diet:	Mother's milk for first 7 months; adults eat berries, meat and fish

WILD FACT

Black bear cubs stay in the den with their mother during the winter months. By late spring they play outside together and learn vital survival skills.

Task 1   Change these ml into litres.

a 2000 ml _____ b 5000 ml _____

c 4000 ml _____ d 9500 ml _____

Task 2   Change these litres into ml.

a 1 litres _____ b 3 litres _____

c 6 litres _____ d $8\frac{1}{2}$ litres _____

Task 3

Change these into litres and ml.

a 3400 ml _____

b 8050 ml _____

Change these into ml.

c 2 litres 6 ml _____

d 7 litres 31 ml _____

Task 4

Write the measures shown on each jug.

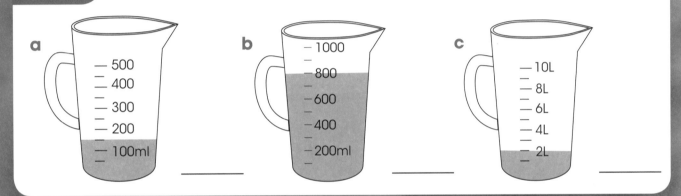

a
— 500
— 400
— 300
— 200
— 100ml

b
— 1000
— 800
— 600
— 400
— 200ml
_____

c
— 10L
— 8L
— 6L
— 4L
— 2L
_____

Exploring Further ...

Write how much milk should be added to or taken out of each bottle to make 750 ml. Make sure you say whether the milk should be added or taken out.

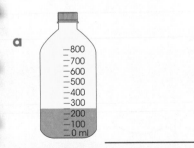

a
—800
—700
—600
—500
—400
—300
—200
—100
—0 ml
_____

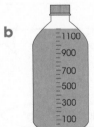

b
—1100
—900
—700
—500
—300
—100
_____

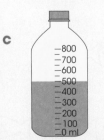

c
—800
—700
—600
—500
—400
—300
—200
—100
—0 ml
_____

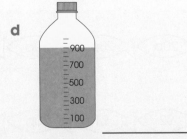

d
—900
—700
—500
—300
—100
_____

Now roar to pages 44–45 to record what you have learned in your explorer's logbook.

27

Money

Being able to deal with money is an important skill.

You need to be able to add and subtract amounts of money.

Are you able to work out *change*?

You should know that there are 100 pence in a pound: 100p = £1

Record your amounts like this:

168p = £1 and 68 pence

205p = £2 and 5 pence

FACT FILE

Animal: Shark pup

Habitat: Wide range of underwater environments

Weight: Great white shark newborns are about 35 kg

Lifespan: Up to 70 years

Diet: Fish and rays

Task 1 — Total each amount in the fish.

a  50p 20p 5p 2p _____

b  20p 10p 10p 5p 1p 1p _____

c  50p 20p 20p 10p 2p 2p 1p _____

d  £2 £2 £1 20p 10p 5p 5p 2p _____

Task 2   A group of friends go to the souvenir shop after a visit to the sealife centre.

Calculate how much each child spends and how much change they each receive.

| 62p | 79p | 35p | 18p | 27p | 95p |

a Sally buys a pencil and two postcards. She pays with £1.

_____

b George buys a pencil, a rubber and a postcard. He pays with £1.

_____

c Alice buys a notebook, a pencil and a keyring. She pays with £2.

_____

d Saima buys a soft toy, a keyring and a pencil. She pays with £2.

_____

e Lee buys two soft toys, a pencil and a rubber. He pays with £5.

_____

WILD FACT

Sharks can have between one and 100 pups.

Exploring Further ...

Scott, Ismail, Beth and Daisy are going on a fishing trip. Scott has £6, Ismail has £5.50, Beth has £4 and Daisy has £4.20 to spend. Before they set off they each buy a snack to take with them. Scott spends £4, Ismail spends £1 and 10p, Beth spends £1 and Daisy spends 70p.
The fishing trip costs £3.

a Calculate how much each child had left after paying for their snacks. _____

_____

b Who can't afford to go fishing? _____

Now glide to pages 44–45 to record what you have learned in your explorer's logbook.

Time

Learn your **time facts!**

60 seconds = 1 minute

60 minutes = 1 hour

24 hours = 1 day

7 days = 1 week

Do you know how many days are in each month?

Thirty days has September,

April, June and November.

All the rest have 31,

Save February alone

Which has 28 days clear

And 29 days in a leap year.

Let's check how well you can tell the time.

FACT FILE

Animal:	Bunny/Kit
Habitat:	Meadows, woods, burrows or domestic habitat
Weight:	25 to 50 g at birth
Lifespan:	2 to 10 years
Diet:	Mother's milk for first 3 weeks, then hay and grass

Task 1   Record the times on these watches in analogue form. Write 'in the morning', 'in the afternoon' or 'in the evening' after each time.

a Jamaal looks at his watch before breakfast.

He says, 'It is _____

_____ '

b Emma looks at her watch just before bed.

She says, 'It is _____

_____ '

c Thomas looks at his watch as he comes out of school at the end of the day. He says, 'It is

3:35

_____

_____ '

Task 2

Record the times on these watches in digital form to the nearest five minutes. Write 'am' or 'pm' after each time.

a  Jake looks at his watch just after breakfast. He says, 'It is nearly

_____'

b  Emma finishes her homework. She says, 'It is way past my bedtime. It is almost

_____'

A newborn kitten cannot see, hear or even crawl during its first week of life. After eight days it can crawl and has fur and, after another two days, it can see.

Task 3

Write true or false.

a January has the same number of days as June. _____

b September has the same number of days as April. _____

c March has one more day than November. _____

d February has twenty eight days in a leap year. _____

In one litter a female rabbit can have up to eight babies and can have up to seven litters each year. This is because survival rates for baby rabbits are very low.

Exploring Further ...

How long does it take each baby rabbit to reach its mum?

	Start time	Finish time		Duration
A	7.40am	10.12am		
B	10 past 8 in the morning	29 minutes past 10 in the morning		
C	7.20am	9.35am		

Now hop to pages 44–45 to record what you have learned in your explorer's logbook.

Angles

An **angle** is created when two lines meet at a point or cross one another.

Acute angle

A square corner, like the corner of a sheet of paper or a book, is called a right angle. You can check whether an angle is a right angle by snipping the corner off a sheet of paper and checking to see if it fits the angle.

Angles allow us to measure turns. You can turn left or right, clockwise or anti-clockwise or use the directions of the compass.

$\frac{1}{4}$ turn

$\frac{1}{2}$ turn

$\frac{3}{4}$ turn

one full turn

WILD FACT

Elephants usually have a single calf at a time. A calf is about 85 cm tall and needs to drink 14 litres of milk each day. In the same way as human babies suck their thumbs, baby elephants suck their trunks.

FACT FILE

Animal: Elephant calf

Habitat: Savannahs, marshes and deserts

Weight: A newborn African elephant weighs 90 to 120 kg

Lifespan: 60 to 70 years in the wild

Diet: Mother's milk until 2 years old, then leaves and fruit

Task 1

Tick the right angles. You may use the square corner of a piece of card to help.

a ☐ b ☐ c ☐

d ☐ e ☐ f ☐

g ☐ h ☐ i ☐

Task 2	Use your knowledge of right angles to make turns.

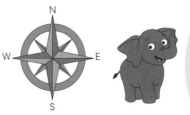

WILD FACT

A female elephant gives birth every four years and can often have two or three calves with her, aged from newborn to 8 or 12 years.

State the compass direction the baby elephant is facing after completing these turns.

a Facing north, make $\frac{3}{4}$ turn to the left _____

b Facing south, make $\frac{1}{4}$ turn clockwise _____

c Facing west, make $\frac{1}{2}$ turn to the right _____

d Facing east, make $\frac{3}{4}$ turn anti-clockwise _____

Task 3	Look at the angles in Task 1. Sort them into the table.

Less than a right angle	Right angle	Greater than a right angle

Exploring Further ...

Help the elephant calves A, B and C to follow the directions to find the correct mum.

a Calf A: Forward 1, $\frac{1}{4}$ turn right, forward 2, $\frac{1}{4}$ turn left, forward 2, $\frac{3}{4}$ turn right, forward 2, $\frac{1}{4}$ turn right, forward 3 _____

b Calf B: Forward 3, $\frac{1}{2}$ turn left, forward 1, $\frac{1}{4}$ turn left, forward 2, $\frac{3}{4}$ turn right, forward 3, $\frac{1}{4}$ turn left, forward 1, $\frac{1}{4}$ turn right, forward 1 _____

c Calf C: Forward 2, $\frac{1}{4}$ turn left, forward 2, $\frac{3}{4}$ turn left, forward 3, $\frac{1}{4}$ right, forward 3, $\frac{1}{4}$ turn left, forward 1 _____

Calf A				Mum 1
Calf B				Mum 2
Calf C				Mum 3
Calf D				Mum 4

Now stomp to pages 44–45 to record what you have learned in your explorer's logbook.

Straight lines

Straight lines are everywhere in the world around us – on our roads, on our houses, in our books. We use lines to help us to describe shapes and they determine the size of angles.

You must be able to recognise when a line is horizontal ____, or vertical |, or somewhere in between ╱

When two lines meet at a right angle, we say they are perpendicular. L

Parallel lines never meet and are equidistant – like railway lines. The lines have the same distance between them right along their length. =

WILD FACT

A baby giraffe is born with horns which are flat against its skull. They straighten up during the giraffe's first week. Very few animals are born with horns!

FACT FILE

Animal:	Giraffe calf
Habitat:	African savannahs, open woodland and plains with tall grass
Weight:	Average newborn weighs 50 kg
Lifespan:	Up to 25 years
Diet:	Mother's milk for up to 12 months but can start eating leaves from 4 months old

Task 1  Say whether the red lines are horizontal, vertical or neither.

a ____ _____

b ╱ _____

c ____ _____

d | _____

e ╲ _____

Task 2   Tick the perpendicular lines.

a

b

c

d

Task 3   Tick the parallel lines.

a

b

c

d

e

f

Exploring Further ...

A _____   B _____

a   On the grid draw:

   i   a line that is parallel to A

   ii   a line that is perpendicular to B.

b   Is your line in **ai** horizontal or vertical? _____

c   Is your line in **aii** horizontal or vertical? _____

Now stride to pages 44–45 to record what you have learned in your explorer's logbook.

2D shapes

A **2D shape** is a flat shape drawn on a piece of paper. They are made up of lines and angles. Sometimes the lines and angles are equal and sometimes they are not. The lines can be straight but sometimes, as in a circle or oval, they are not.

Check which shapes you can name and see whether you can describe them properly. The first thing to check is how many lines a shape has.

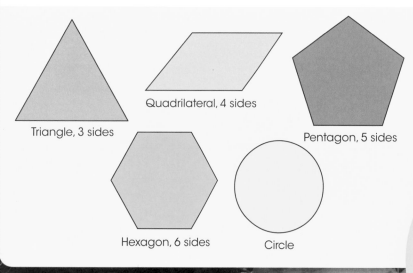

Triangle, 3 sides

Quadrilateral, 4 sides

Pentagon, 5 sides

Hexagon, 6 sides

Circle

Task 1   Complete these shapes to make:

a a quadrilateral with equal sides.

b a triangle with one right angle.

Task 2   A quadrilateral is a shape with four sides. Sort these shapes into the table.

Quadrilateral	Not a quadrilateral
	A,

Task 3   Sort the shapes in Task 2 according to the number of right angles.

No right angles	1 right angle	2 right angles	4 right angles
A,			

WILD FACT

Despite the mother watching over her young for a few weeks longer, only one out of every ten crocodile babies make it to adulthood.

Exploring Further ...

Look again at shapes A–M in Task 2.
Sort them now by the number of right angles AND equal sides.

	Some equal sides	No equal sides
One or more right angles		
No right angles	A,	

Now swim to pages 44–45 to record what you have learned in your explorer's logbook.

3D shapes

A **3D shape** has a length, a width and a depth, which can all be measured.

3D shapes can be described by how many **surfaces** (**faces**) they have. Most 3D shapes have **corners** (**vertices**) and **edges**.

You should be able to name and describe the following shapes:

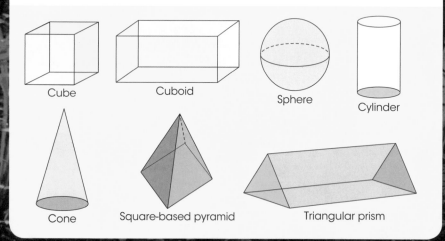

Cube   Cuboid   Sphere   Cylinder

Cone   Square-based pyramid   Triangular prism

Task 1   Here are some pictures of everyday objects. Match the picture to the shape.

    cuboid

    cylinder

   cone

    sphere

Task 2 What are the names of the shapes on the ends of these prisms?

a _____

b _____

c 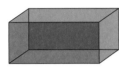 _____

d _____

Task 3 Complete the table below.

Shape	Faces	Edges	Vertices
Square-based pyramid			
Cylinder			
Pentagonal prism			
Hexagonal prism			

WILD FACT

Gorillas, chimpanzees, orangutans, gibbons and bonobos are apes. Baby apes are born in a nest. They can crawl by two months and walk by eight months.

WILD FACT

Apes are excellent parents, carrying their babies around everywhere for the first few months and displaying great affection towards them. Babies stay with their mothers for six or seven years. Fathers teach them vital survival skills.

Exploring Further ...

Here is a model made of a cuboid and a triangular prism.

How many:

a faces _____   b edges _____   c vertices _____

does it have?

Now roam to pages 44–45 to record what you have learned in your explorer's logbook.

Statistics

Statistics deal with information. In maths we call information **data**. Data is presented in different ways. On this page you can discover and investigate **tables, pictograms** and **bar charts**.

Task 1

Jenny recorded the weights of the lambs born on Cherry Tree Farm.

Weight of newborn lamb	Number of lambs
Less than 4 kg	6
4 kg or more to 5 kg	12
5 kg or more to 6 kg	28
6 kg or more to 7 kg	30
7 kg or more	14

a How many lambs were born on Cherry Tree Farm altogether? _____

b How many lambs were born weighing less than 5 kg? _____

c How many lambs were born weighing 7 kg or more? _____

d How many fewer lambs were born weighing 6 kg or over than those weighing below 6 kg? _____

FACT FILE

Animal: Lamb
Habitat: Grasslands, mountains and farms
Weight: 2.2 to 4.5 kg
Lifespan: 10 to 12 years
Diet: Mother's milk for first 60 to 70 days, then grain-based foods

Task 2 Johnny counted the types of dogs in his puppy training class.

Border collies	🐶 🐶 🐶
Alsatians	🐶 🐶
Labradors	🐶 🐶
Poodles	🐶
Mongrels	🐶 🐶 🐶 🐶

🐶 = 2

a How many of the puppies were border collies? _____

b How many more labradors were there than poodles? _____

c How many puppies were there altogether? _____

d How many puppies were not mongrels? _____

Exploring Further ...

Krysti counted the types of baby apes she saw at the local zoo and recorded them in a bar chart.

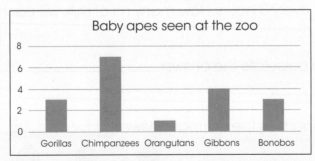

Baby apes seen at the zoo

(bar chart: Gorillas 3, Chimpanzees 7, Orangutans 1, Gibbons 4, Bonobos 3)

a How many chimpanzee babies did she see? _____

b Which two types of ape had the same number of babies?

_____

c How many more gibbon babies were there than orangutan babies? _____

Now skip to pages 44–45 to record what you have learned in your explorer's logbook.

Quick test

Now try these questions. Give yourself 1 mark for every correct answer – but only if you answer each part of the question correctly.

1 Partition these numbers:

342 = ☐ hundreds + ☐ tens + ☐ units

2 Put these weights in order, starting with the heaviest first.

238 g   328 g   228 g   218 g   283 g   282 g   281 g

_____

3 Foal A's legs measure 85 cm. They will grow a further 9 cm. Foal B's legs measure 118 cm and will grow a further 15 cm.
Whose legs will be longer when fully grown and by how much? _____

4 Five years ago there were 55 nesting pair of eagles in Norland. This year 18 nesting pairs were counted. How many more pairs were there five years ago? _____

5 A swan swam down the canal for 465 m. It then swam back up the canal for 249 m. How far did it have to swim to get back to where it started? Show your working.

6 Sort the following numbers into multiples of 3 or multiples of 4.

16   8   6   18   27   33   28   20   21   32

3: _____   4: _____

7 A hoglet needs 4 ml of milk every 3 hours. How many ml of milk will each hoglet drink in 24 hours?

Show the sums you used to calculate the answer. _____

8 8)456   Which duckling has the correct answer? _____

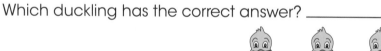

9 Put a ring round $\frac{3}{10}$ of these seal pups.

42

10 Kai wants to fence his rabbit run. Calculate the perimeter to help him decide how many metres of fencing he needs. _____

3 m

600 cm

11 Jenny has to feed an orphan bear cub 35 ml of milk every 4 hours. How much milk does she need for 24 hours? _____

12 How many 1p coins would I need to buy a pair of binoculars costing £7 and 7p?

_____

13 What is the time difference between Clock A and Clock B?

_____

4:25

A   B

14 The elephant must follow these directions to reach the water hole. Put a cross in the square where the water hole is.

Forward 3. Make $\frac{3}{4}$ turn anti-clockwise. Forward 2.
Make $\frac{1}{4}$ turn left. Forward 1. Make $\frac{1}{2}$ turn clockwise.
Forward 4.

15 State whether each labelled angle in this quadrilateral is a right angle, more than a right angle or less than a right angle.

a _____   b _____

16 Use the graph to answer the question.

How much taller is the giraffe than the elephant? _____

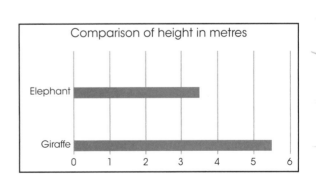

Comparison of height in metres

Elephant

Giraffe

0   1   2   3   4   5   6

Explorer's Logbook

Tick off the topics as you complete them and then colour in the star.

Addition ☐

Mental subtraction ☐

Subtraction ☐

Numbers up to 1000 ☐

Place value ☐

Multiplication ☐

Mental addition ☐

Multiples ☐

Division ☐

Time ☐

Money ☐

Weight ☐

Length ☐

Fractions ☐

3D shapes ☐

2D shapes ☐

Angles ☐

Straight lines ☐

Capacity ☐

Statistics ☐

45

Answers

Pages 2-3
Task 1
a 2 units = 2   b 5 hundreds = 500
c 9 tens = 90   d 6 units = 6
e 5 tens = 50   f 3 hundreds = 300

Task 2
a 56   b 27   c 628   d 304

Task 3

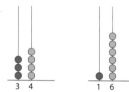
3 4

1 6

4 5 0

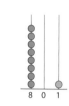
8 0 1

Exploring Further...

	Hundreds	Tens	Units	
150		1	6	166
540		5	7	597
610		7	1	681
320	4	4	3	763
430	2	2	8	658

Pages 4-5
Task 1
a forty-three   b ninety-one
c two hundred and fifty-eight
d seven hundred and seven

Task 2
a 77   b 618   c 999

Task 3
a 545 540 504 454 450 405
b 11 101 110 111 121 211

Task 4
a 169 170 171 172 173 174
b 581 591 601 611 621 631

Exploring Further...
a 873   b 378   c 783

Pages 6-7
Task 1
a 858   b 680   c 963   d 313
e 231   f 719   g 907   h 370

Task 2
a 482   b 196   c 300   d 444
e 662   f 559   g 384   h 842

Task 3
a 881   b 901   c 936   d 903

Exploring Further...

208	965	160	17	395	58	471	178	36	47	729	28	653
909	398	492	56	824	25	57	93	97	798	74	30	67
27	48	86	593	92	77	54	149	91	207	772	229	41
643	81	741	19	62	482	87	150	903	712	797	845	78
45	68	88	663	303	999	697	6	85	505	228	99	37

Pages 8-9
Task 1
a 761   b 807   c 714   d 929
e 762   f 511   g 392   h 283

Task 2
a 195   b 312   c 350   d 301

Task 3
a 608   b 65 days   c 44

Exploring Further...
a 83 and 62, 33 and 54   b 37
c 33   d 54

Pages 10-11
Task 1
a 85   b 179   c 89   d 101

Task 2
a 965   b 329   c 310   d 605

Task 3
491

Exploring Further...
a 364 + 47 + 258 = 669   b 497 + 306 + 83 = 886
c 59 + 327 + 109 = 495

Pages 12-13
Task 1
a 806   b 912

Task 2
a 27   b 45   c 32   d 331

Task 3
a 285   b 570   c 211   d 39

Exploring Further...
a 27 cm   b 48 cm

Pages 14-15
Task 1
a 18, 20, 22, 24, 26, 28, 30, 32
b 18, 21, 24, 27, 30, 33, 36, 39
c 16, 20, 24, 28, 32, 36, 40, 44
d 15, 20, 25, 30, 35, 40, 45, 50

Task 2
a 20, 60, 30, 100   b 24, 48, 80, 96
c 8, 48, 32   d 12, 30
e 50, 60, 10   f 100, 200, 600

Task 3
a 30   b 72

Exploring Further...
a Tadpole 1 becomes Frog C
b Tadpole 2 becomes Frog A
c Tadpole 3 becomes Frog B

Pages 16-17
Task 1
a **i** 6	**ii** 15	**iii** 12	**iv** 18
b **i** 18	**ii** 20	**iii** 16	**iv** 22
c **i** 28	**ii** 40	**iii** 56	**iv** 24

Task 2
a 672   **b** 150

Task 3
a 445   **b** 296   **c** 184   **d** 282

Task 4
a 480   **b** 320   **c** 350   **d** 200

Exploring Further...
a 7 cm × 4 = 28 cm   **b** 6 cm × 5 = 3 cm
c 4 cm × 5 = 20 cm

Pages 18-19
Task 1
a **i** 12	**ii** 6	**iii** 10	**iv** 9
b **i** 6	**ii** 8	**iii** 3	**iv** 12
c **i** 7	**ii** 8	**iii** 7	**iv** 8
d **i** 9	**ii** 6	**iii** 4	**iv** 7

Task 2
a 20	**b** 30	**c** 30	**d** 60
e 100	**f** 200	**g** 20	**h** 175

Task 3
a 34	**b** 31	**c** 42
d 20	**e** 23	**f** 13

Exploring Further...
Sandwiches 4   Apples 2
Grapes 8   Packet of crisps $\frac{1}{2}$
Biscuits 1

Pages 20-21
Task 1
a Shaded: three-tenths $\frac{3}{10}$
     Unshaded: seven-tenths $\frac{7}{10}$
b Shaded: eight-tenths $\frac{8}{10}$
     Unshaded: two-tenths $\frac{2}{10}$

Task 2
a $\frac{3}{6}$ $(\frac{1}{2})$ **b** $\frac{8}{12}$ $(\frac{2}{3})$

Task 3
a $\frac{1}{2} > \frac{1}{3}$ **b** $\frac{1}{4} > \frac{1}{5}$ **c** $\frac{1}{8} < \frac{1}{6}$ **d** $\frac{2}{7} < \frac{2}{3}$

Exploring Further...
a $\frac{9}{12}$ $(\frac{3}{4})$ **b** $\frac{6}{9}$ $(\frac{2}{3})$

Pages 22-23
Task 1
a 3 cm   **b** 7 cm   **c** 10 cm   **d** 4 cm

Task 2
a 12 mm   **b** 3 cm   **c** 8 cm

Task 3
a 36 cm   **b** 173 cm   **c** 33 cm

Exploring Further...
4 cm	duckling	40 mm
150 mm	kitten	15 cm
50 cm	seal pup	$\frac{1}{2}$ m
20 mm	tadpole	2 cm
2 m	giraffe	200 cm
100 cm	elephant	1 m

Pages 24-25
Task 1
Gram: cygnet, hoglet, newborn joey
Kilogram: foal, fawn, baby elephant

Task 2
a 1 kg	**b** 2 kg	**c** 7 kg	**d** 3 kg
e 6 kg	**f** 4 kg	**g** 6000 g	**h** 5000 g
i 500 g	**j** 2000 g	**k** 1000 g	**l** 7000 g

Task 3
6 kg, 4 kg, 3500 g, 2000 g, 1400 g

Exploring Further...
a 2020 g = 2 kg 20 g   2002 g = 2 kg 2 g
     2200 g = 2 kg 200 g   2202 g = 2 kg 202 g
     2220 g = 2 kg 220 g   2022 g = 2 kg 22 g
b 557 g + 402 g + 141 g = 1100 g
c

Pages 26-27
Task 1
a 2 litres   **b** 5 litres   **c** 4 litres   **d** $9\frac{1}{2}$ litres

Task 2
a 1000 ml   **b** 3000 ml   **c** 6000 ml   **d** 8500 ml

Task 3
a 3 litres 400 ml   **b** 8 litres 50 ml
c 2006 ml   **d** 7031 ml

Task 4
a 150 ml   **b** 800 ml   **c** 2 litres

Exploring Further...
a Add 500 ml   **b** Take away 450 ml
c Add 250 ml   **d** Take away 150 ml

Pages 28-29
Task 1
a 77p   **b** 47p
c £1 and 5p   **d** £5 and 42p

Task 2
a Spent 71p	29p change
b Spent 80p	20p change
c Spent £1 and 76p	24p change
d Spent £1 and 92p	8p change
e Spent £2 and 52p	£2 and 48p change

Exploring Further...
a Scott £2   **b** Scott
     Ismail £4 and 40p
     Beth £3
     Daisy £3 and 50p

Pages 30-31

Task 1

a quarter past 8 in the morning.

b quarter to 9 in the evening.

c twenty five minutes to 4 in the afternoon.

Task 2

a 7.20am   **b** 9.45pm

Task 3

a False   **b** True   **c** True   **d** False

Exploring Further...

A 2 hours 32 minutes

B 2 hours 19 minutes

C 2 hours 15 minutes

Pages 32-33

Task 1

a, **f** and **i** are right angles

Task 2

a east   **b** west   **c** east   **d** south

Task 3

Less than a right angle	Right angle	Greater than a right angle
c, d, h	a, f, i	b, e, g

Exploring Further...

a Calf A = Mum 1   **b** Calf B = Mum 3

c Calf C = Mum 4

Pages 34-35

Task 1

a horizontal   **b** neither   **c** horizontal

d vertical   **e** neither

Task 2

a and **d** ticked

Task 3

b and **d** ticked

Exploring Further...

a   i   ii

b horizontal   **c** vertical

Pages 36-37

Task 1

a   **b** or

Task 2

Quadrilateral	Not a quadrilateral
C, F, G, H, J, K	A, B, D, E, I, L, M

Task 3

No right angles	1 right angle	2 right angles	4 right angles
A, B, E, G, H, I, J, M	L	D, K	C, F

Exploring Further...

	Some equal sides	No equal sides
One or more right angles	C, F	D, K, L
No right angles	A, B, G, H, I, J	E, M

Pages 38-39

Task 1

ice cream cone: cone   football: sphere

cereal packet: cuboid   toilet roll: cylinder

Task 2

a hexagon   **b** pentagon

c rectangle / square   **d** square

Task 3

Shape	Faces	Edges	Vertices
Square-based pyramid	5	8	5
Cylinder	3	2	0
Pentagonal prism	7	15	10
Hexagonal prism	8	18	12

Exploring Further...

a 7 faces   **b** 15 edges   **c** 10 vertices

Pages 40-41

Task 1

a 90   **b** 18   **c** 14   **d** 2

Task 2

a 6   **b** 1   **c** 23   **d** 15

Exploring Further...

a 7   **b** gorillas and bonobos   **c** 3

Answers to quick test

1 342 = 3 Hundreds + 4 Tens + 2 Units

2 328g 283g 282g 281g 238g 228g 218g

3 Foal B's legs will be longer by 39cm

(133cm – 94cm = 39cm)

4 37 more pairs

5
$$4\ ^56\ ^15$$
$$-\ 2\ 4\ 9$$
$$\overline{\ \ 2\ 1\ 6m}$$

6 3: 6, 18, 27, 33, 21

4: 16, 8, 28, 20, 32

7 24 ÷ 3 = 8

4ml × 8 = 32ml

8 57   **9** 3 pups ringed   **10** 18m

11 210ml   **12** 707   **13** 8 hours 10 minutes

14

🐘			
X			

15 a right angle   **b** less than a right angle

16 2m